Forces

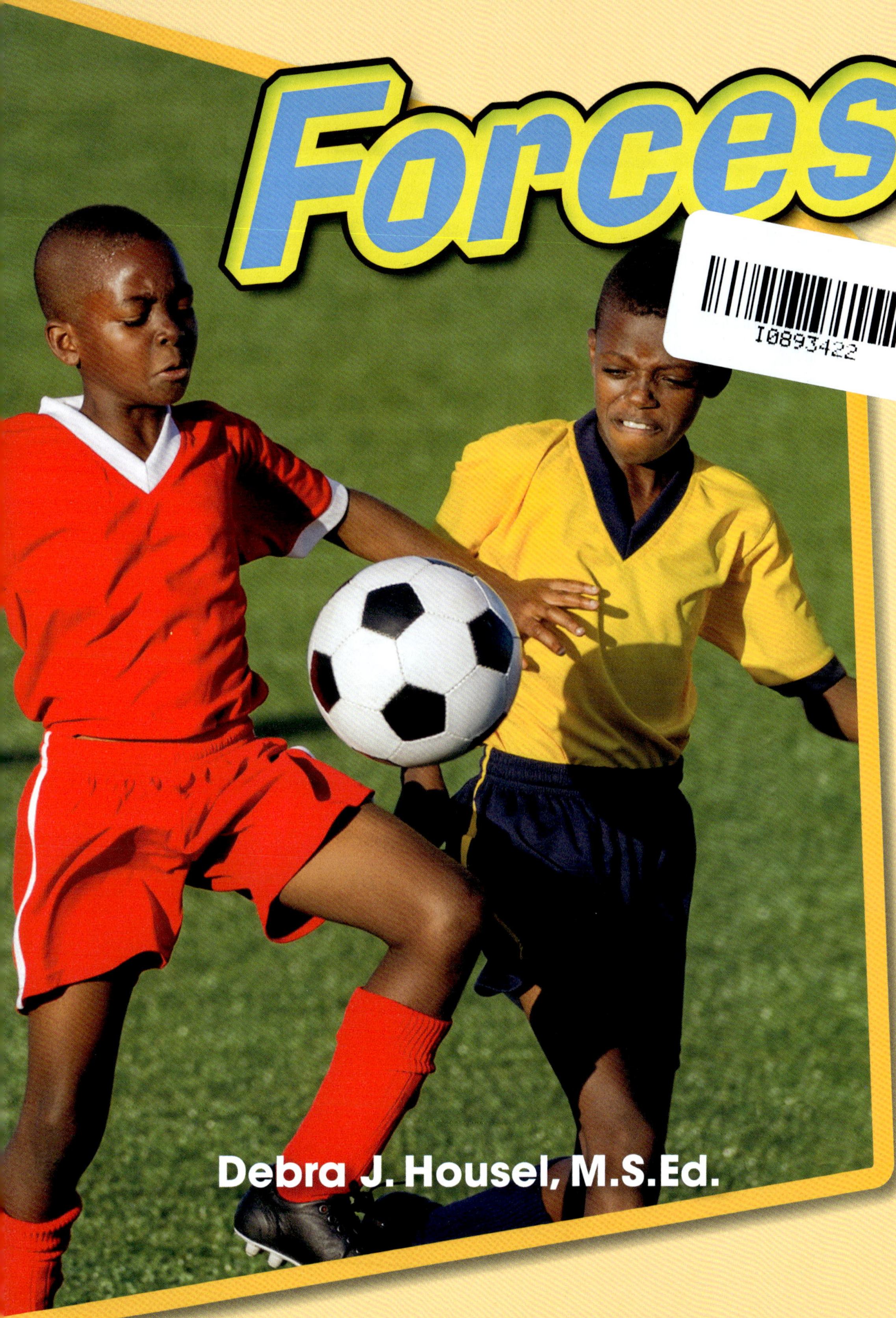

Debra J. Housel, M.S.Ed.

Consultants

Sally Creel, Ed.D.
Curriculum Consultant

Leann Iacuone, M.A.T., NBCT, ATC
Riverside Unified School District

Image Credits: Cover & p.1 iStock; p.27 (bottom) Blend Images/Alamy; p.26 (top) Buzz Pictures/Alamy; p.19 (top) PhotosIndia.com LLC/Alamy; p.19 San Jamar (bottom); pp.20–21 (background) Bryan and Cherry Alexander/ Science Source; pp28–29 (illustrations) Janelle Bell-Martin; all other images from Shutterstock.

Library of Congress Cataloging-in-Publication Data

Housel, Debra J., author.
Forces / Debra J. Housel, M.S.Ed. ; consultants, Sally Creel, Ed.D., curriculum consultant, Leann Iacuone, M.A.T., NBCT, ATC Riverside Unified School District, Jill Tobin, California Teacher of the Year semi-finalist Burbank Unified School District.
pages cm
Summary: "There are forces acting on your body right now. Every time you breathe and move, forces are used. Gravity is the force that stops us from flying into outer space. Without forces, we would not be able to move!" — Provided by publisher.
Audience: K to grade 3.
Includes index.
ISBN 978-1-4807-4604-6 (pbk.)
SBN 978-1-4807-5071-5 (ebook)
1. Force and energy—Juvenile literature. I. Title.
QC73.4.H68 2015
531.6—dc23

2014014112

Teacher Created Materials
5301 Oceanus Drive
Huntington Beach, CA 92649-1030
http://www.tcmpub.com

ISBN 978-1-4807-4604-6

Printed in China 51497

Table of Contents

Forces Are All Around

Your lungs use force to pull air when you breathe in. They push air when you breathe out. You use muscle force to turn your head. But what is force?

A force is a push, a pull, or a turn. Every force has an equal and opposite force. When you sit, you put force on a chair. This force is your weight. The chair pushes back with equal force. Its force is the strength of the materials from which it is made.

Forces are always with you!

These forces are balanced.

As the girl jumps, the trampoline pushes back with equal and opposite force.

What Forces Do

A force can make something move. A push or a pull can open a door. As you eat, you pull the fork up to your mouth. A push can bring the fork back to your plate.

A force can make something stop moving, too. A golf ball will roll along the ground. But it won't roll forever. Why? The ground exerts a force against the ball. This stops the ball.

What if there was no force? Once the ball started moving, it would just roll and roll and roll.

You cannot see forces. Yet they are always at work. A force can make a moving thing go faster. If you are coloring and move your hand faster, the crayon speeds up. A force can slow something down. When you want to stop a swing, you drag your feet on the ground. A force can make something change direction, too. If you are playing soccer, you kick the ball. This makes the ball go in a different direction.

All of these kids are using forces.

Gravity

Gravity is a force that pulls all things toward one another. **Mass** affects gravity. The bigger something is, the more gravity pulls on it.

Weight measures how hard gravity pulls on an object. As you get older, you get bigger. Gravity pulls on you more, so you weigh more.

The moon is smaller than Earth. It has less gravity. So, if you went to the moon, you would weigh less!

The moon's gravity pulls on Earth's oceans. This is what causes high and low tides.

How much does it weigh on . . . ?		
	Earth	**the Moon**
	55 pounds	9 pounds
	8 pounds	1 pound
	3,500 pounds	583 pounds

Without gravity, there would be no life on Earth. Planets would not revolve around the sun. They would just float through space.

Life on Earth starts with the sun. The sun is huge. Its gravity is very strong. It holds Earth and all the other planets in their **orbits**. This keeps the planets from smashing into one another!

The planets orbit the sun.

With gravity, size matters! The moon's gravity is weak compared to Earth's. And Earth's gravity is weak compared to the sun's.

The moon orbits Earth.

Friction

Friction is also a force. Friction gives things grip. It is what lets your hand hold a doorknob so you can turn it. It is what lets you walk, rather than slide, on a sidewalk.

Friction slows motion. It does not let things slip or slide smoothly. The moving parts on a bike are oiled to reduce friction.

These shoes increase friction, so you won't slip when you walk.

Whenever two things touch each other, there is friction. Sometimes, there is very little friction. There is very little friction when you glide across ice on ice skates.

Sometimes there is a lot of friction. As you ride your bike, the tires press against the ground. The ground also presses against the tires. You pump the pedals to keep moving. If you stop pumping, the bike slows and then stops. Friction makes this happen.

Finger Friction

Your fingertips have ridges so you can grip things. When soap fills these ridges, it is hard to hold things.

Magnetism

Magnetism (MAG-ni-tiz-uhm) is a force. It makes certain types of metal **attract** or **repel** other metals. These metals are magnets. A magnet's two ends are called poles. One is its north pole. One is its south pole.

A magnet's north pole will always attract, or pull close, another magnet's south pole. The south pole of a magnet will always repel, or push away, another magnet's south pole. Two north poles will also repel each other. The area around a magnet is called a *magnetic field*.

Heavy Metal

Steel and iron are magnetic metals. They can also be very heavy. So people use giant magnets to move them.

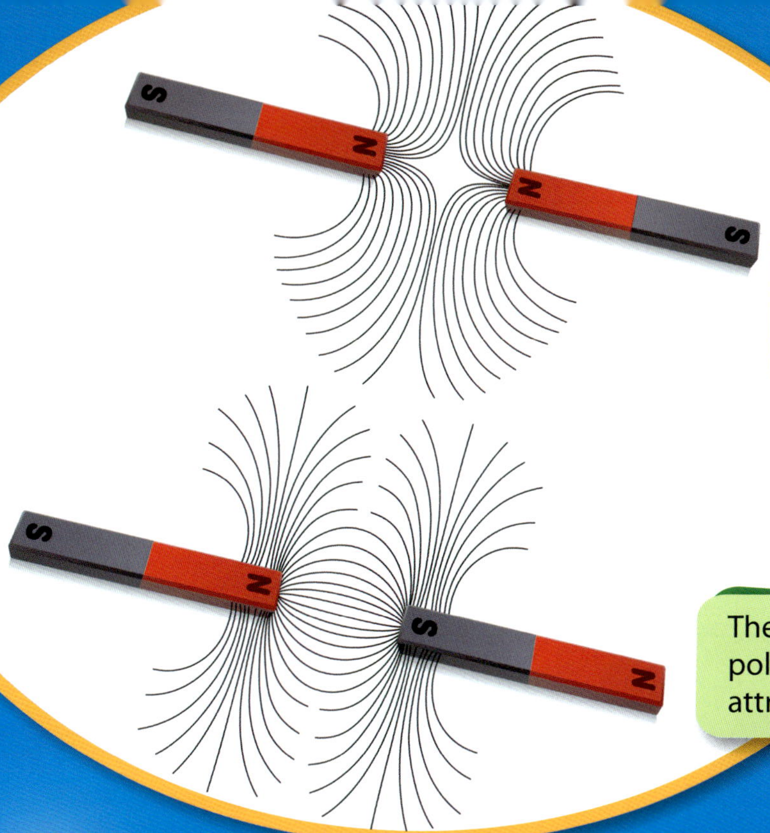

The north poles of these magnets repel each other.

The north and south poles of these magnets attract each other.

Some restaurants use trash cans that have magnetic lids so forks and knives don't get thrown away. Knives that have touched the special lid become magnetic and can pick up forks and spoons.

There are many types of magnets. Earth is a giant magnet. A compass needle is also a magnet. It always points to Earth's north pole. This is why you can use a compass to figure out where you are. It works anywhere in the world, even in the middle of an ocean. If you spill a box of paper clips, you can quickly pick them up with a horseshoe magnet. The paper clips will be attracted to the magnet. They will cling to it.

The magnetic north pole of Earth is not actually at the North Pole. It is a little south of the North Pole.

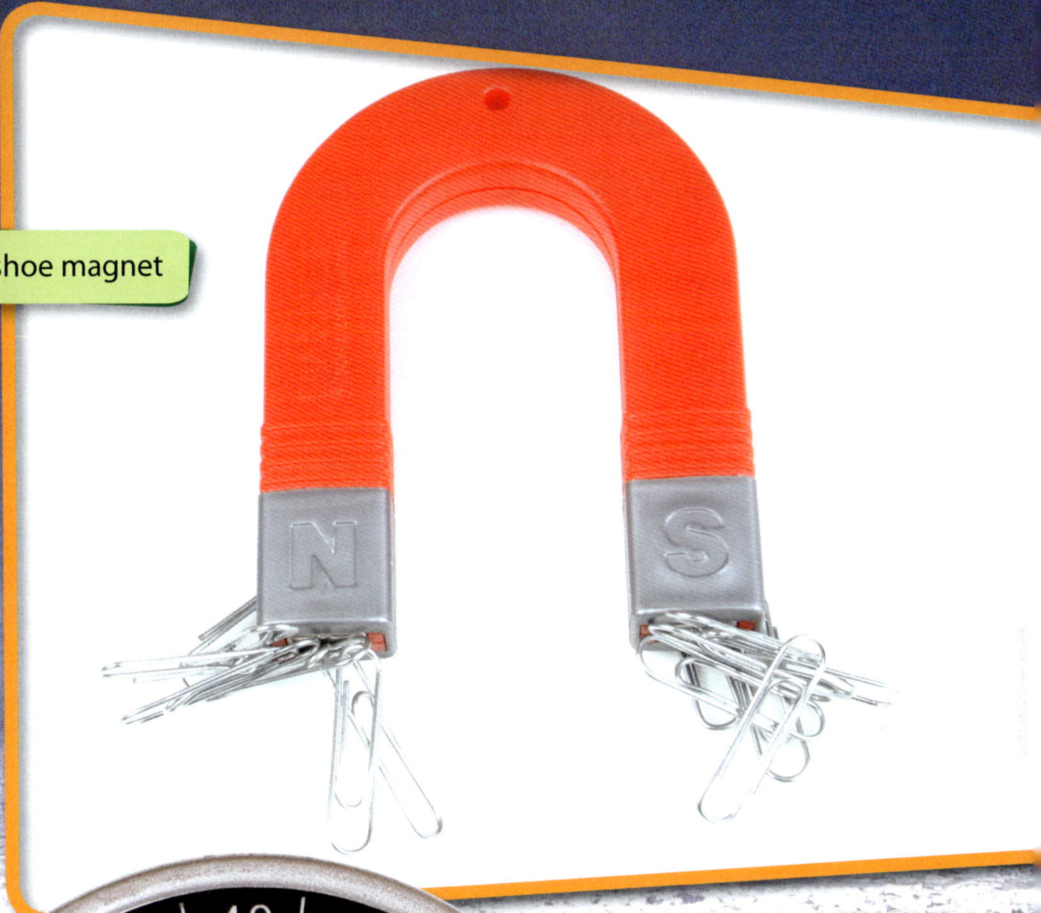

horseshoe magnet

compass

Buoyancy

When you take a bath, you do not fill the tub to the top. You know that when you step in, the water level will rise. You **displace** some of the water with the mass of your body.

This girl floats because there is enough water to displace her mass.

You cannot float in your tub. You do not displace enough water to float. But you can float in a pool or a lake. There is a lot more water to hold you up. This floating force is called **buoyancy**.

This dog does not float because there is not enough water to displace his mass.

When you drop a pebble into a pond, it sinks to the bottom. Yet large ships float. What causes some things to float and others to sink? The answer is buoyancy.

Buoyancy depends on water displacement. For a thing to float, it must displace an amount of water that weighs *more* than itself. Ships are designed to displace a large amount of water. They are hollow and full of air.

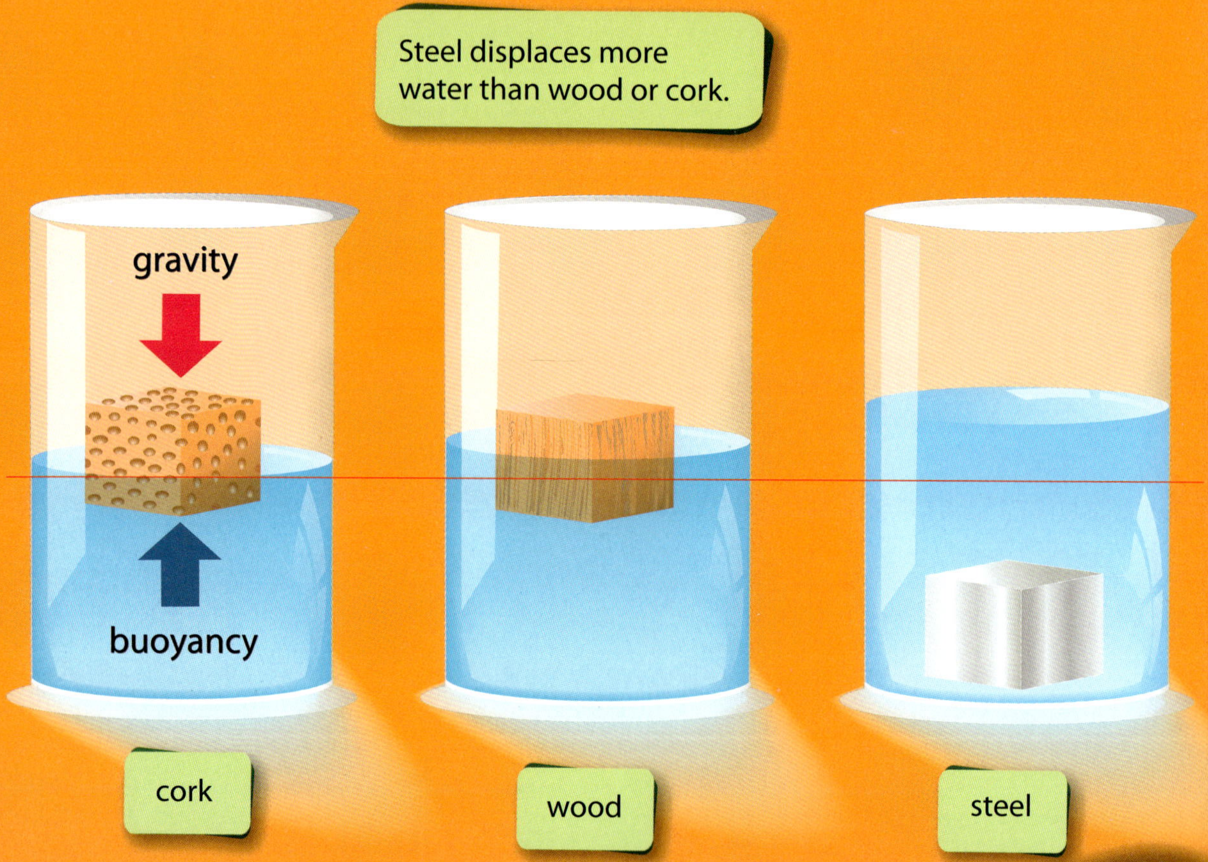

This ship is very large. It must displace a lot of water in order to float.

Plimsoll Lines

Cargo ships have Plimsoll (PLIM-suhl) lines on their sides. They mark the lowest level at which a ship will float.

Forces in Your Life

You come into contact with forces each day. Sometimes a force works against you. Gravity works against you when you have to push hard to ride your skateboard up a hill. At other times, forces help you. Gravity helps you slide down a hill on a sled. Magnets help you hang things on a fridge. Friction helps you turn fast in a soccer game. Buoyancy helps you float in a pool. Whether forces work against you or help you, they are always with you!

Friction keeps this skateboard under control.

Magnetism helps this girl show off her artwork.

Let's Do Science!

What forces can you find? See for yourself!

What to Get

- balloon
- large pail
- water

What to Do

1. Fill a large pail about two-thirds full with water.

2. Blow up the balloon and tie it closed.

3. Push the balloon gently into the water. Let go. What happens?

4. Push the balloon all the way to the bottom of the bucket. Let go and stand back! What happens?

5. What did you notice? Draw and label pictures to show what forces were at work.

Glossary

attract—to cause something to move closer

buoyancy—the force of a liquid that makes things float

displace—to move something out of its original position

friction—a force that slows motion

gravity—a force that causes things to fall toward Earth

magnetism—the pull between certain metals

mass—the amount of matter (material) in something

orbits—the curved path that something follows as it goes around something else

poles—the ends of a magnet

repel—to keep something out or away

Index

Your Turn!

Just Like Magic!

Put some paper clips on a cookie sheet. Move a strong magnet under the cookie sheet. What happens? What kind of force is at work? How far away can you hold the magnet and still see it move the paper clips? What else can you do with magnets?